YOUR LITTLE BOOK OF WISDOM

Reflections on Living an Inspired Life

Kathryn L Kaplan, PhD

Christmas Lake Press

Published by Christmas Lake Press 2025

www.christmaslakecreative.com

Copyright © 2025 by Kathryn L Kaplan, PhD

ISBN 978-1-960865-40-3

All rights reserved. No part of this publication may be reproduced, stored in a retrieval system, or transmitted in any form, or by any means, electronic, mechanical, photocopying, recording, or otherwise without the prior permission in writing of the copyright holder, nor be otherwise circulated in any form or binding or cover other than the one with which it was originally published, without a similar condition being imposed on the subsequent publisher.

Interior layout by Daiana Marchesi

YOUR LITTLE BOOK OF WISDOM

To my two sisters and dearest friends
who lovingly appreciate and nourish
wisdom in our daily lives

Contents

Introduction	1
Perspective	13
Feelings	21
Aspirational Distinctions	31
Trusting Yourself	41
Authorizing Yourself	51
Relationships	61
Healing	71
Grieving	83
Keeping a Journal	95
Vulnerability Is Strength	111

Introduction

In 2023 I surprised myself by publishing two memoirs. The first I'd been wanting to write for a long time but hadn't known where or how to begin; the second started with an ending I hoped I'd never have to write. To say I poured my soul into both would be no exaggeration, and after finishing the second book—a grief memoir on the loss of my beloved husband of thirty years—I had pretty much nothing left. I was spent. And yet... the universe was nudging me to do more—in this case, put another book out into the world. A *third* book. And when the universe nudges, I've learned I have to listen.

Though I resisted at first, having no energy, no sense of why this new book mattered, and plenty of reasons to procrastinate—eye surgery, a conference, traveling to see friends, completing my end-of-life documents, moving to a new house—this book kept insistently asking, even demanding, despite all my rationalizations, to be created. And the request wasn't just coming from the universe at large. After reading both my memoirs, dear friends who know me well sent me quotations—*my very own words*—that had informed, inspired, comforted, consoled, cajoled, convinced, or convicted them, with comments such as, "Wow," "Whew," "A head shaker," "A gem," "Great question," and, "Me too." They not only encouraged but urged me to capture these essential nuggets from my deep and detailed research and writing in a "little book of quotations," a sort of modern commonplace, so that those who might benefit could dive right into them without wading through the deep waters of narrative.

For the uninitiated, a commonplace book is a journal or notebook (a scrapbook prototype), used since antiquity and especially during the Renaissance for collecting and organizing interesting or useful information—such as quotations, ideas, observations, or other passages—for later reference and reflection. Remember, the iPhone Notes app has only been around since 2007! A commonplace serves as a personal repository of knowledge, a memory aid, and a source of inspiration. Though I hadn't thought about it, my friends seemed to believe that my collection of wisdom was "uncommon."

Still, those of you who know me won't be surprised that I put this project aside—for a year—before bringing my full self to it. No amount of encouragement was enough to make me feel my own connection to a book of *my* wisdom. After all, how wise was I, really? And who was *I* to write it? I looked with awe at some of my role models who have written about wisdom and exhibit wisdom in all they say and do, and I saw myself coming up short. Point one: Even though I knew how helpful my words had been to *me*, I doubted they were profound enough to help others in a significant way. Point two: I lacked the experience and stature of my exemplars in this area—Maria Popova, author of *The Marginalian*; Krista Tippett, host of the *On Being* podcast; and Parker Palmer, a prolific writer and educator. Point three: I did not have an online platform with thousands or even hundreds of followers.

I know comparison to others is unfair, dangerous, and self-demeaning. Theodore Roosevelt called it "the thief of joy." But it's natural to measure ourselves against those we esteem. So how did I get over my impostor syndrome and get unstuck? Drawing on a lesson I learned from one of my doctoral committee mentors over thirty years ago, I decided to "authorize myself." And that meant I didn't need anyone else's sign-off or approval. Only *I* could give myself permission to write from my experience, and even though I'm not as well-known, established, connected, and followed, I'm *allowed* to be me.

In Palmer's April 23, 2025, interview with Tippett, they spoke about how you don't have to be famous to be wise. They noted how often someone would refer to a grandparent, teacher, or neighbor who profoundly touched them with their presence and care, having a significant impact on their life. Those influencers (the real kind) were not famous. Therefore, I don't have to be famous to share what is meaningful to me. As I myself once said, "I am an excellent mirror for others, and that fills me with genuine satisfaction."

In Popova's reflections (from October 23, 2024) on eighteen years of writing *The Marginalian*, she explains that she writes to metabolize her life and to note what she needs to learn and relearn. When she or others—parents, poets, philosophers, clergy, or therapists—provide guidance, you realize that no matter how valuable the wisdom, "in the end, you discover that you make the path of life only by walking it with your own two feet." If we take Popova's perspective to heart, these sentiments are true for you the reader and for me the writer.

As I finally got ready to begin writing, I found myself wondering, what exactly is wisdom? The *Cam-*

bridge Dictionary defines it as "the ability to use your knowledge and experience to make good decisions and judgments." In other words, wisdom encompasses understanding, common sense, and insight, often leading to actions that are both prudent and effective. Essentially, it's the practical application of knowledge and experience to navigate life's complexities.

My three role models put it more eloquently:

Palmer emphasizes that wisdom comes from listening to one's life, embracing paradoxes, and recognizing the interconnectedness of all things.

Popova has said that "Living wisely is the art of learning how you will wish to have lived."

In *Becoming Wise: An Inquiry into the Mystery and Art of Living* (2016), Tippett writes, "I have seen that wisdom emerges precisely through those moments when we have to hold seemingly opposing realities in a creative tension and interplay: power and frailty, birth and death, pain and hope, beauty and brokenness, mystery and conviction, calm and buoyancy, mine and yours."

I think it makes sense to define wisdom as pretty much anything that helps you make a better choice. Here are some additional quotations about wisdom that helped me get going.

"We are not what we know but what we are willing to learn."

—Mary Catherine Bateson,
cultural anthropologist

"Pass on what you have learned."

—Yoda,
Star Wars: The Last Jedi

"Vulnerability is seen as a gateway to wisdom."

— attributed to Rumi

"The highest form of wisdom is kindness."

—*The Talmud*

Finally, mind-body medicine expert Joe Dispenza suggests that "a memory without the emotional charge is called wisdom." This sounds a lot like Wordsworth's "emotion recollected in tranquility," which implies that great poetry results not from a sudden burst of emotion but thoughtful and calm reflection on past emotional experience. Dispenza's take is that when one can recall a past experience without being overwhelmed by the emotions associated with it, they have achieved a level of understanding or perspective that can be considered wisdom.

With these guiding quotations, I was ready to forge ahead, and I hope you are, too.

Your Little Book of Wisdom is designed to be a companion, to accompany you when you need it—and even to let you *know* when you need it. You'll want this book on your nightstand, in your purse or briefcase, your glove compartment or backpack—or all of the above. You'll find if you carry it with you, maybe in digital form on your smartphone or tablet, it will, in turn, carry *you* through the highs and lows, the joyful moments and rough spots, the times when you are looking for something wise to say to someone or need some wise advice yourself. You may be feeling flat and need a nudge to get going. Or perhaps you would benefit from some inspiration to help you aspire to more than you can currently conceive. Whatever the case, I know there have been countless times over the years when I would have loved to have so much wisdom all in one place, easy to access, there to remind me of what I have forgotten or never knew.

Many of the quotations you will find here (attributed to "KK") are drawn from my two memoirs, *Becoming Visible to Myself* and *Dying with His Eyes Wide Open*. Writing these books was a healing process that allowed me to come to terms with who I really am and, subsequently, with loss and grief. An avid journal keeper, I decided to review all thirty-two of my spiral-bound notebooks—my commonplaces, each crammed with quotations, notes, collages, and sketches—in a manner both methodical and energized by heartfelt curiosity. This "both/and" approach led to many new insights. I had always seen my journey as one of seeking—searching for integration. Little did I know, rereading my own journal entries could provide a felt sense of self-trust and growing confidence. I was reminded that others had felt what I felt, expressed what I struggled to express, and felt compelled to share their discoveries in a way that would be helpful. They provided the stepping stones, and now I was, in my own way, expanding the path.

I also couldn't have foreseen that finishing my first book would end with an epilogue about my husband's diagnosis of cancer and death eight months later. Nor did I expect to be transformed by that loss and find my purpose and passion as a thanatologist—a death, dying, and bereavement specialist. In my wildest dreams, I never imagined I would write about *that* experience to console and counsel others similarly grieving loss. Though grief work is now my focus, quotations on grief constitute only one section of this book, and are meant to apply to many, if not most, of the challenging situations we face. After all, suffering is universal.

The format of this book is intended to make it easy for you to find just the right thought, right when you need it. You can flip to the section that matches your current quest. You can also open the book to a random page and see what message is there for you.

The content is predicated on *less is more*. There is no attempt to be inclusive or provide the last word on wisdom. Instead, these quotations are selected because they have been significant to me, and I hope they will be inspiring, thought-provoking, motivating, and useful for you.

The categories are subjective. As a qualitative researcher by training, I start from the ground up—the quotations themselves—and let them suggest the theme they represent. Likewise, the quotations told me what order they wanted to appear in. I wrote introductions to each section to set the context for the material that follows. I deliberated with many of the quotations because they could fit in several places. My bottom line was to ask myself, in what mood or circumstance would these words be a salve and/or a guiding light?

Make no mistake, some of these urgings may have you "Swimming with the Sharks" (the title of one of many "poem portraits" from my 1994 original research on thirty-two successful women who worked as organization development consultants). In other words, it can be difficult to take actions that are going against organizational or familial norms. You may not at first be ready for the repercussions. But that doesn't mean you are bad or wrong or even not ready. Discomfort brings growth, and growth is a spiral process, not a straight arrow.

Other times you may be mulling over these deep insights, but not inclined to take immediate action. That's OK. Marinating in these awarenesses may be exactly what you need. In a society of short attention spans, digital absorption, and bias toward fast action, you may be seen as—and feel—out of step, like an outlier. But as one of my categories suggests, "Trusting Yourself" is imperative. Get to know your soul's longing and heart's desire. Then follow that thread wherever it leads you. I call that voice "my deepest, wisest self." My intention is to write something that is engaging and touching. I hope that what you find here resonates with you and fulfills a need you may not have known you had. May this book support you and enrich your journey of listening to yourself in a sensitive, attentive, and loving way.

> Kathryn L Kaplan
> June 2, 2025

Perspective

Some wisdom comes in the form of declarations and definitions. But these statements are frequently just the tip of the iceberg of a lifetime of research, professional experience, and deep knowledge. The author of the quotation has a point of view, and if you follow it, you may reap rewards and benefits in your own life.

When I was diagnosed with retinitis pigmentosa (RP), a progressive eye disease that often results in blindness, I actually thought my condition was punishment for not having perspective growing up. *Seriously*. The symptoms of RP are decreased peripheral vision, night blindness, and impaired depth perception. The analogy to not seeing myself, my surroundings, and my life clearly was easy to grasp. Eventually, I had to stop driving and start using a cane when walking. Going down stairs that have no contrast, like those on the New York subway, was treacherous for me and irritating to others. I have had to adapt, at first painfully—and the process continues.

The antidote to a narrow field of vision, metaphorically and literally, is to look around. Read what others have learned and written. Watch movies, listen to podcasts, and think about things outside of your usual way of knowing and acting. In other words: Open your eyes.

For me, having perspective sounds like a drum roll. The curtain goes up and something new and exciting is about to begin. Though many of these quotations may come across as prescriptive, I want you to read them as descriptive of the author's perspective, from which you can take what makes sense for you and leave behind what doesn't. There is wisdom here, depending on how you look at it. Embrace it, play with it, and make it your own.

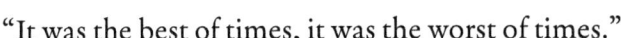

"It was the best of times, it was the worst of times."

—Charles Dickens, *A Tale of Two Cities*

"The two most important days in your life are the day you were born and the day you find out why."

—attributed to Mark Twain

"Live the questions now. Perhaps you will then gradually, without noticing it, live along some distant day into the answer."

—Rainer Maria Rilke,
Letters to a Young Poet, trans. M.D. Herter Norton

"The quality of light by which we scrutinize our lives has direct bearing upon the product which we live, and upon the changes which we hope to bring about through those lives."

—Audre Lorde,
"Poetry Is Not a Luxury"

"Life gets simpler when you know yourself."

—one of my past therapists

"People say that what we're all seeking is a meaning for life... I think that what we're seeking is an experience of being alive, so that our life experiences on the purely physical plane will have resonances within our own innermost being and reality, so that we actually feel the rapture of being alive."

—Joseph Campbell, *The Power of Myth*

"The past is just a story we tell ourselves."

—Samantha, the AI operating system in *Her*

"Everything has a shelf life, including life itself."

—one of my past therapists

"Tidying sentimental things means putting the past in order."

—Marie Kondo

"Things do not always go according to plan; people are not loving and loyal all the time; pain is part of life; everything changes and ends; and life is not always fair."

—my past grief therapist, for RP and more

"Things may be difficult, but not impossible."

—a motto that a neighbor, the parent of a child with a severe eye disorder, shared with me

"It is only with the heart that one can see rightly: what is essential is invisible to the eye."

—Antoine de Saint-Exupéry,
The Little Prince, trans. Katherine Woods

Feelings

My biggest yearning has been "to have my life with me in it." I wanted "to live before/until I died." That meant making friends with those unwanted sensations and intuitions—those things called feelings—that didn't make *logical* sense to me. It also meant stopping my attempt to numb my feelings by burying myself alive with overwork.

Emotional intelligence provides a way to *think* about our feelings in order to make good decisions, take effective actions, and enjoy healthy relationships. But sometimes we just have a meltdown and can't think straight. We collapse into younger parts of ourselves and can't climb out of the dark hole. Someone says something, we get triggered, and before we know it, we are reexperiencing a past memory and don't realize it.

Floundering, we react from a wounded part of ourselves, often hurting the person on the other end. Getting angry, we lash out, tired of blaming ourselves for our misery, and wanting to avoid accountability. We may then be ashamed of ourselves in the aftermath as we examine the impact of our less mature selves on others.

In addition, ignoring our feelings is not surgical; we cannot just block out the bad ones. Our connection to the flipside—happiness, joy, fulfillment, arousal, tenderness, even love—gets hijacked, and we are often not aware that we have lost access to these sensations. We simply feel . . . anxious, stuck, depressed.

When selecting the quotations below, my focus was on getting in touch with discomfort and overcoming it. Mysterious clues that something is amiss or needs further deliberation can baffle us, and our tendency is to banish these thoughts in order to uncomplicate our life. That is where poets and sages come in with counterintuitive advice. Welcome them!

Some psychotherapists suggest "disidentifying" with the parts of yourself that aren't your true essence. This was easier said than done for me, especially when I would tell myself, "I'll never get what I want, nothing helps, I'm a wreck, I can't get to the bottom of it, and I hate myself and my life." The most fundamental change in my life occurred when I became willing to name and accept *all* my feelings—the good, the bad, and the ugly.

The Appendix of *Becoming Visible to Myself* is an annotated list of my recommended tools and resources. However, for inspiration to jumpstart your own inner wisdom, try these quotations on for immediate connection—and reconnection—to your true self.

"What got you here won't get you there."
—Marshall Goldsmith

"This being human is a guest house.
Every morning a new arrival.

A joy, a depression, a meanness,
some momentary awareness comes
as an unexpected visitor.

Welcome and entertain them all! . . .

The dark thought, the shame, the malice,
meet them at the door laughing
and invite them in.

Be grateful for whoever comes,
because each has been sent
as a guide from beyond."

—Jalaluddin Rumi, "The Guest House,"
trans. Coleman Barks

"When I dare to be powerful—to use my strength in the service of my vision, then it becomes less and less important whether I am afraid."

—Audre Lorde

"Vulnerability is a strength."

—KK

"When we share intense emotions, their energy is like a tuning fork: it resonates with similar emotions in the person listening to us. In themselves, listening to us stirs up unpleasant/disturbing waves in their psyches. Their attempt to 'help us feel better' may, more likely, be seen as their attempt to shut down the feelings in us that are resonating unpleasantly in them so that *they* can feel better."

—Robyn Posin

"If you can spot it, you've got it."

—my cousin's psychotherapist

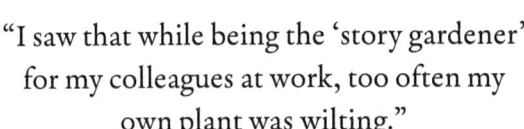

"I saw that while being the 'story gardener' for my colleagues at work, too often my own plant was wilting."

—KK

"What we have named as anger on the surface is the violent outer response to our own inner powerlessness, a powerlessness connected to such a profound sense of rawness and care that it can find no proper outer body or identity or voice, or way of life to hold it."

—David Whyte

"My little one inside needs a 'good mommy voice.' When I treated HER, my undamaged core, with love and patience, then I had an invincible partnership. When I treated HER as I was treated as a child—with disdain, disgust, and impatience—then she didn't feel safe, and I sabotaged her through accidents, illness, mess, and excess weight."

—KK

"When overwhelmed, focus on the smallest slice of now."

—Robyn Posin

"I had two parts that always needed to be heard and held: my big in-the-world self and my scared little one inside who always says, "I can't." These were my light and my darkness, and they never go away, so they both needed tending."

—KK

"I may not be there yet, but I am closer than I was yesterday."

—Misty Copeland

Aspirational Distinctions

My default mode once I started my working life was to beat myself up for mistakes, compare myself unfairly to colleagues, and essentially un-motivate myself. One day a friend said, "I always hear about what you can't do and why—what about all the things you CAN do?" What a concept! This became the seed for being attracted to what I call "aspirational distinctions." These consist of quotations and good advice that make a distinction between two or more aspects, largely taking the form "this vs. that." With this new tool under my belt, my default mantra whenever

I was down and doubting myself became "What CAN I do?"

This positive and constructive way of talking to myself energized me to make decisions (something I found difficult) and achieve more. "I can't afford the vacation I wish I could have, but I can go to the Caribbean." "I didn't publish my dissertation when I wanted to, but I can write about my journals from a qualitative research point of view now." One of the women in my study taught me the distinction between when to rest and when to push through.

After my husband died of cancer, being a caretaker could no longer be my identity. So what *could* I do? In the beginning, I just needed to feel my feelings without falling permanently into a dark hole. After a while, our palliative care physician, Dr. Alma, became my mentor and encouraged me to track my grieving process and use my experience to become a thanatologist. She recommended I attend the same thirteen-month program she did to become a grief therapist—even though it was online (due to COVID) and in Spanish! (I lived in Mexico at the time.) What *could* I do? Take a deep breath, cross my fingers, and commit.

Sometimes we need to aspire to something beyond what we think is possible. Being stuck in a rut, judging ourselves in comparison to our contemporaries, or doubting our capacity to change can all impact our level of achievement and satisfaction. But have you ever imagined a little birdie whispering in your ear, "You could do more. You could *be* more. You are not alone."

Think of the people you know, and the biographies you've read of individuals who have stepped up and out, who made a contribution beyond anything you would have expected of them or that had been done before. Do you harbor a secret wish inside of you to invent something, start a new business, move to a new country, or express yourself creatively? Nourish those clues, keep yourself safe, and give consideration to the parts of yourself you don't know as well.

These quotations embody distinctions that might just urge you to take another step, path, or risk. They may introduce ideas you haven't thought of, which somehow ring true. They may jolt you out of complacency. Chew on them.

"Don't let what you can't do blind you to what you can."

—attributed to Helen Keller

"Success is stumbling from failure to failure with no loss of enthusiasm."

—attributed to Winston Churchill

"Why spend the majority of your professional life working on *tolerable* stuff for *acceptable* clients when ... you can spend your days working on exciting things for interesting people?"

—David Maister

"If you could say it in words, there would be no reason to paint."

—Edward Hopper

"You cannot cross the sea merely by standing and staring at the water."

—Rabindranath Tagore

"You can't see the picture when you're in the frame."

—Les Brown

"Learn how to die and you will learn how to live."

—Mitch Albom, *Tuesdays with Morrie*

"I have come to believe over and over again that what is most important to me must be spoken, made verbal and shared, even at the risk of having it bruised or misunderstood."

—Audre Lorde, "The Transformation of Silence into Language and Action"

"There are two ways of spreading light; to be the candle or the mirror that reflects it."

—Edith Wharton, "Vesalius in Zante"

"The meaning of life is to find your gift. The purpose of life is to give it away."

—David Viscott

"Life can only be understood backwards; but it must be lived forwards."

—Søren Kierkegaard

"Do I prefer to grow up and relate to life directly, or do I choose to live and die in fear?"

—Pema Chödrön

"My life does not have meaning because of my work, but my work has meaning because my life has meaning. My own imminent approaching death . . . is always whispering, 'What has this day counted for?'"

—KK, Poem Portrait

Trusting Yourself

Just as I was writing this section, a friend called. She had planned to attend a silent retreat but was having second thoughts. Quieting herself as we talked it through, she heard from what I call her "deepest wisest self." The advice? "You need to go on the retreat." Though this wasn't necessarily logical, she regrounded herself, got centered, and was willing to trust herself once more.

Trusting ourselves takes such courage. It means paying attention to bodily sensations and honoring uncomfortable emotions. Sometimes trusting yourself feels slippery and hard to hold on to. Other times it's like a sledgehammer. Being willing and committed to "feeling it all," presents our best chance of hearing, absorbing, and acting on our best guidance and wisdom.

I remember several experiments I undertook to figure out how to trust myself. As a child I felt I needed to be a good girl, follow my parents' rules, and use achievement to make *them* look good. In college, I noticed the world was so much larger than the small frame I grew up in. One day I sat down on a bench in the university courtyard, pen and paper on my lap, and started listing all the options and topics I could think of relating to what I could do with my life. The list kept expanding out and out, like a mind map (before I even knew what one was), and I felt totally overwhelmed. I quickly decided this approach was not profitable for me.

Then, after I completed my PhD, I fell into a dark hole. I had loved the academic environment and the mentoring that helped me far exceed my own expectations—and my advisors'. For once I not only achieved for myself, but also experienced the joy of deep satisfaction. Missing that ten-year journey, and not having a clue what to do next, I took to my bed. I decided to stay there until a real motivation emerged. Then, after months of not sensing any new direction, my best friend, a psychotherapist, became alarmed and referred me to a psychiatrist for antidepressants. Out of bed and taking meager steps into the world, I started to work and found a context where I could at least survive.

I suppose experiments are considered viable even if the results are a failure. I concluded that my failed outcomes were a result of not knowing how to make decisions. I then read about pros and cons, logic and emotions, intuition and facts, to no avail. I wanted a repeatable process and a feeling of certitude that worked for me. Little did I know that I was searching for how to trust myself. What I finally discovered through journaling over many years was that I had multiple selves inside of what was considered "me" and my identity. I was less worried that I might be schizophrenic, and more afraid of not knowing the truth of who I was and what I wanted. By getting to know each part of myself and asking these parts their names and what they knew, felt, and wanted, I was able to piece together my wholeness. I realized I wanted integration and I could bumble and stumble to achieve it with lots of mini-experiments, not one big "Aha!"

While the facts of your life and your journey of self-discovery are unique to you, you might identify with the impetus to trust yourself. What I am offering is permission to do your own mini-experiments to find what is true for you in an embodied way. These quotations may nudge you in the direction that fits your inner and outer needs.

"Don't waste energy trying to be something you're not. Being true to yourself is the essence of finding your voice—lead by letting it ring true."

—Sally Helgesen, *The Female Advantage: Women's Ways of Leadership*

"While I'm searching for what I'm missing, I'm missing my life."

—a past spiritual therapist

"I can tell you that what you're looking for is already inside you."

—Anne Lamott

"I am ever deepening my relationship to myself—I look inside for meaning to my life. I reach and stretch for my soul's longings. I let myself get all the help my precious being needs. I realize that to be vulnerable is a strength. And I believe in risking being real over and over."

—KK

"Faith is taking the first step even when you don't see the whole staircase."

—Martin Luther King, Jr.

"Climbing out of a box bigger than you are isn't just hard—it's impossible. You have to break down the walls, not by demolishing them but by realizing they exist only in your imagination, or more accurately, your lack thereof."

—KK

"If you had stayed with him, you would be like a tree that grew crooked. You need to see that everything you felt with him was already inside you. Rather than cheat yourself by using his energy to complete you, you could find the wholeness in yourself over time."

—one of my past therapists

"Let reality be your teacher. Trust you're not alone. Have faith in yourself and how you cope."

—KK

"Be the diva you truly are, not the eternal ingenue."

—my "old girls' network"

"Give it the time it needs.
Trust your inner compass."

—KK

> "Be someone who lives to her edge
> and from her center."
>
> —KK

> "I am in constant contact with my soul's longing
> and my heart's desire, and that, yes that, is enough."
>
> —KK

"Dying isn't hard, not living fully is."

—KK

Authorizing Yourself

One of my doctoral committee mentors challenged me by asking, "When are you going to authorize yourself?" Huh? I had no idea what she meant. Doesn't authority come from *outside* yourself? Perhaps this possibility, to authorize yourself *yourself*, is as foreign to you as it was to me when I first heard the term. Did my mentor think I could do things I didn't think I could? Was she saying I could do original research, teach, and contribute to the academic field already? That I was *ready*? My filter was that I wasn't equipped or ready. I was told repeatedly growing up that I "wasn't allowed"—to wear stockings, have a boyfriend, or . . . fill in the blank. Therefore, I assumed my mentor must have been annoyed with me and impatient because of my deficiencies. I was convinced—like the Scarecrow, the Cowardly Lion, and the Tin Man—that I needed *her* to give me a brain, courage, and a heart. But it turned out, she was waiting for me to see what she could see and take up the mantle on my own initiative. Like Dorothy in *The Wizard of Oz*, I realized I didn't need her to wave her magic wand to go home to myself. She knew I had the capacity inside me all along—I just had to click my heels three times. She was advocating for me to finally step up, take risks, use my talents, excel, and be the real me. She enabled me to realize that it was up to me to value and empower myself, to realize that only I can be the author of my life. Her reframe was a priceless gift that I want to extend to you.

So what exactly is authorizing yourself? It is a process that looks different in each individual's life. It can develop step by step in small to large moments of courage and insight. My first foray into this awareness was in a dream. Rather than my usual black or white way of thinking, I saw an image of me digging down into the dirt of my soul to get more material to integrate and bring into the light. I awoke with a felt shift in my view of how I could deal with life differently.

Standing up to authority while respecting your own, making yourself visible with colleagues, or skillfully holding your own during tense meetings are all forms of authorizing yourself. One of the most significant examples with my parents was when I heard them on the phone not sounding like themselves. They had hastily decided to sell their house and go into assisted living. It sold in one day, surprising them, and the sudden pressure to move had them a mess—sounding depressed, anxious, confused, and in conflict. Usually my dad got angry if anyone offered help, so I spoke from my heart. "I hope you don't get mad at me, but I ache for you and Mom. I feel like I could help. I want to see you. Would that be OK?" He responded tenderly and uncharacteristically, "I'm touched. When are you coming?!" I flew the next day from New York to California and made a difference in their dynamic and plans. It was the beginning of our role reversal and it was just right. I didn't need their permission to use my perceptions and act on them. Authorizing myself was the key, and it can unlock many other doors throughout life for you.

"I will never regret taking the high road and staying focused on all the good things my parents gave me."

—KK

"Owning our story and loving ourselves through that process is the bravest thing that we will ever do."

—Brené Brown

"At my best, I am a 'story gardener' who plants seeds and cultivates the soil so others can grow to their full potential and heal."

—KK

"Your beautifully messy complicated story matters (tell it)."

—Kelly Rae Roberts

"When you can let yourself really accept who and how you are . . . no one else will have much problem with it. Practice letting yourself just be."

—Robyn Posin

"I was here, and here's my story."

—Dani Shapiro, *Still Writing: The Perils and Pleasures of a Creative Life*

"'My pain is my purpose': a way to turn my difficult experience into my special offering, authorizing myself with my secret sauce."

—KK

"Your abyss is not your angst; that's the reality of your life circumstances because you're a daring woman; and you work on things ahead of which there are real abysses."

—Peter B. Vaill, private correspondence

"My mantra for not getting overwhelmed or ahead of myself: Know where you are and be where you are. Later, when working full-time in my new career, I added: Know who you are and be who you are."

—KK

"It doesn't interest me if the story you are telling me is true. I want to know if you can disappoint another to be true to yourself; if you can bear the accusation of betrayal and not betray your own soul."

—Oriah Mountain Dreamer, "The Invitation"

"Instead of beating myself up for not producing paintings and poetry, I saw that my work, relationships, and projects were also a form of art. In other words, 'my life was my palette.'"

—KK

Relationships

My mother and I had a complex, often conflicted, and at times painful relationship. On her deathbed we spoke of forgiveness, and achieved—not without effort—peaceful closure. From conception to death, we have many opportunities to learn and grow from our varied relationships. They are not black and white because we are not just one thing or the other, love or hate. We embody a broad and multifaceted range of feelings. But with curiosity, patience, wise counsel, and aspiring to stretch ourselves, we can rise to truths and understandings that matter.

In your own life, how often do you hear people say, "Why can't we just get along?" If only it were that easy. We are all so different, and yet if we look carefully, we also have so much in common. When we encounter polarized views on a topic, such as politics or religion, it can be hard to listen. We instinctively reject what we do not like or do not understand. It is easier to put up a wall and defend our position with righteous indignation than to try to put ourselves in the other person's frame of mind.

With partners, we want to be intimate, but half of us get divorced. Siblings often grow up learning roles that lead to jealousy and competition, causing family rifts. Our unexamined assumptions play out in similar ways at work. The Golden Rule says to treat people the way you want to be treated. But other research, such as the Platinum Rule, suggests treating people the way *they* want to be treated.

Narcissists want everything their way. Codependents are happy to give that to them, at their own expense. Bullies find victims who are easy targets. Mediators try to get everyone to own their part, but it doesn't always work. Power trumps empathy. Compassion is often perceived as weakness. Being human—vulnerable—is frowned on. Visible strength is envied. These are all patterns that must be owned and broken.

We have so much to admire and learn from each other, and from the generations that came before us. But how often to do we take advantage of that wisdom? The starting point is humility—honoring ourselves *and* other*s*.

Though it seems like it should come naturally, relationship savvy is a learned skill. When I worked in medical centers, we created a program to value and teach mutual respect. We had a physician leadership curriculum that involved learning to negotiate and build teams. We acknowledged that we needed allies and mentors to be successful. No one is a rock or an island. We cannot make it through life alone.

"You are like a Mercedes with the brakes on. When are you going to take them off?"

—a past boss

"To live in the hearts of those you love is never to die."

—Hazel Gaynor

"Not all relationships are about growth. Sometimes they are just about loving people for who they are and adjusting expectations and investment accordingly."

—Katherine Woodward Thomas

"I only said one sentence to you and you reacted way out of balance. What button just got pushed?"

—a question from a leadership coach

"Legacy isn't necessarily about greatness, but simply about the impact people have while they're still here. Released from this quest, I could leave my legacy to the hearts and minds of people I may have inspired and influenced."

—KK

"Understanding someone's suffering is the best gift you can give another person. Understanding is love's other name. If you don't understand, you can't love."

—Thích Nhất Hạnh, *How to Love*

"Just as flowers bloom when they are ready and in their unique splendor, people blossom when given the right type of care, conditions for success, and consistent attention in any weather."

—KK

"It takes two people to have a relationship and only one to end it."

—a past couples therapist

"If you hate a person, you hate something in him that is part of yourself. What isn't part of ourselves doesn't disturb us."

—Hermann Hesse, *Demian*

"The unspoken deal is this: If you will bury the parts I don't like, then I will love you. The unspoken choice is this: Lose yourself or lose me."

—Judith Viorst

"I accept it all as part of the real and messy life and love that is mine."

—KK

"I continue to feel angered by friends whom I feel don't know me or seem to care to. I am willing to let go of a friendship if it turns out I am not visible to them, because I am now becoming visible to myself."

—KK

Healing

When I was in my forties, during the one-two punch of getting divorced and getting a PhD, I asked every woman I interviewed for my dissertation a question that was not part of my study. I desperately wanted to know if there had ever been a point where these successful consultants felt totally confident and satisfied—essentially "there." From the outside, they all appeared to me to have arrived. But to a person, all thirty-two were adamant that life is a journey, not a destination—that, in effect, there was no "there." This helped me to understand that on the journey, we suffer emotional injuries and wounds and that healing from these is not an end point but a continuous process. I was chagrined and disappointed, but also relieved. Thinking they had achieved perfection, I had wanted to be one of them. Seeing them as they saw themselves—imperfectly perfect—freed me to be more myself.

Once I became an organization development consultant, like them—at least by profession—I understood even more about what they had told me. I learned that conflict at work—among departments, between managers and their staff, and on teams—did not have a nice, neat resolution. In other words, it couldn't be fully healed. Leaders and individuals bumbled and stumbled to make substantial improvements, even with admonitions to get better results and guided by skilled facilitation. Further, the complex inequities of race, gender, age, and socioeconomic status made changing an organization's culture fraught with unconscious bias and prejudice. It was a process. It was messy. And it was the only way to bring about change.

Perhaps you have grappled with this question in your work life: How does one heal an institution, society, or government? Understanding the question in the context of process rather than outcome provides the answer. Wounds don't heal and people don't change at the pace or in the way we want them to. Progress takes time. As Martin Luther King, Jr. said, "The arc of the moral universe is long, but it bends toward justice." Systemic racism will almost surely never be healed in America, but we can keep making things better if we try. And a large part of the healing comes from *knowing* we are trying.

Back to the workplace for a moment, and how people change. Colleagues may have differences in styles and competencies. You may reflect on your original family and the culture in which you grew up as it relates to what you're experiencing at work. You observe the choices you are making to create your own family, friends, and financial freedom.

Then something happens, out of the blue, that knocks you off your feet. Your sense of coping on your own is challenged. It could be a disaster, such as your house burning down. Or you may face a chronic illness in yourself or loved ones. For me, when I was laid off from my position as a vice president, I felt humiliated and betrayed. Although I handled the logistics of leaving responsibly and with dignity, my identity and sense of self were shattered. Having time—for once—I went to the Lighthouse Guild for training in low vision to prepare for possible blindness from RP.

What my counselor there said surprised me. After several sessions, she told me that, even worse than my eye problem, and more damaging than my shame about losing my job, was my lack of awareness that I was unconsciously enmeshed with my parents and how they treated me as a child. She said it was time for me to face and grieve my lack of a healthy childhood. Luckily for me, she was empathic and wise enough to help me do it. And how ironic that a counselor for blindness helped me see in this way!

This is true healing: when you get to the root cause of your patterns and are guided to find another way to your spiritual home. The quotations I have chosen here might just give you a wake-up call to go deeper, get the best therapy and help possible, and do the hard but necessary work of growing up, getting more whole, and fulfilling your potential.

"Healing is coming to terms with things as they are."

—Jon Kabat-Zinn, *Letting Everything Become Your Teacher*

"Healing may not be so much about getting better, as about letting go of everything that isn't you—all of the expectations, all of the beliefs—and becoming who you are."

—Rachel Naomi Remen

"As long as we take ourselves to be the child who was hurt by an unconscious parent, we will never grow up."

—Geneen Roth, *Women Food and God*

"The thing that is really hard, and really amazing, is giving up on being perfect and beginning the work of becoming yourself."

—Anna Quindlen

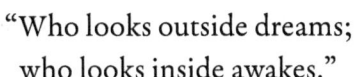

"Who looks outside dreams;
who looks inside awakes."

—Carl Jung

"The real voyage of discovery consists not in seeking new landscapes but in having new eyes."

—paraphrased from Marcel Proust,
Remembrance of Things Past

"You need only claim the events of your life to make yourself yours. When you truly possess all you have been and done, which may take some time, you are fierce with reality."

—Florida Scott-Maxwell, *The Measure of My Days*

"Only by circling around the same issues again and again can the therapist identify your patterns and make helpful interpretations and recommendations."

—KK

"Visualize two ice floes. In order to avoid falling into the freezing water, picture yourself leaping from one (the old behavior) to the other (the new desired behavior)."

—Robyn Posin

"Turn your wounds into wisdom."

—Oprah Winfrey

"To understand how slow the process of change can be and how many tiny, hard-to-see micromovements are required, picture a large cruise ship in the process of making a 180-degree turn."

—Robyn Posin

"The final stage of healing is using what happens to you to help other people."

—Gloria Steinem

"The journey to self-discovery has its own rhythm and pace."

—KK

Grieving

Before my husband of thirty years died of cancer, it seemed to me we would just keep going, adapting to each indignity and moving on together as always. But death is a turning point. Grief is messy, personal, unique, and full of sorrow.

At first I was sleepwalking, in shock, trying to process why I was still here and he wasn't. The torture of him being gone was that I had been so devoted to taking care of him, it became who I was. So who was I now? How could I take care of myself? What would be my purpose?

It's one thing to know logically what to do to keep healing, it's another for your heart to accept the grief and face the tremendous loss. Only after doing this could I appreciate the gift of having had someone know you as you really are, warts and all. But the idea that someone's absence could become a daily and sustaining presence—which I was learning as I began studying grief therapy—was something I hadn't thought before and couldn't even imagine. This passage from my second memoir, *Dying with His Eyes Wide Open*, sums it up:

> Patrick is gone, but I am ever so grateful to have had someone worthy of my grief and to have had the love we shared for thirty years. It is time to move forward—I know this—but it will take all my strength, courage, and love to find my way on a circuitous path that only I can walk.

Grief permeates so many of the elements in this book: perspective, feelings, healing, relationships. If I hadn't kept notes in my journal, the whole experience would have been a blur. I trusted my impulse to learn to draw Patrick realistically, in both words and black-and-white lines, to metabolize the loss.

Grieving, for me, is a journey of becoming whole when it seems impossible because daily companionship with your beloved is gone. The emotions are what connect our hearts, not the circumstances. My commitment was to keep his love, our memories, and his wisdom inside of me each day. To tell myself I am not alone. I am not starting over. I am going forward in a new way, emboldened by our relationship.

I can say from my experience that it is important to linger in grief and respect your ambivalence, to feel it all, even if it's old, boring, irritating, or illogical. Being left and having to navigate life without your beloved is universal. The particular case of who you lost and who you are now is the tricky part, and can't be scripted in advance. You are not one nor two, but a third presence, the relationship between you, which continues through loving.

I felt I should have been more mature as the caregiver, but sometimes we just triggered each other. I admit that I begrudged dear friends who are still couples. At one point I wondered, "Am I allowed to be, dare I say it, happy?" Dr. Alma asked me three powerful questions: How was I feeling now? What do I most miss? What do I need? These helped me reset.

Death is one of those turning points where you can gain a new perspective, act differently going forward, and authorize yourself to tell your story—your truth, your way. Death is a great teacher; don't miss the opportunity to learn from it.

"You're killing me. It's not your fault. You didn't mean to abandon me. But I'm dying here."

—KK

"Everyone has the only death they can."

—Dr. Alma Huerta, palliative care and thanatology

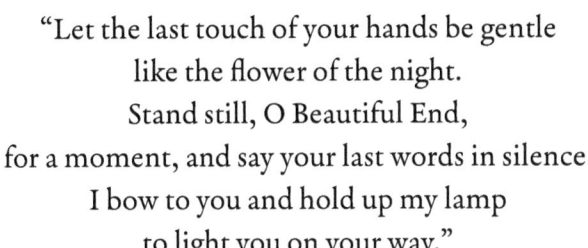

"Let the last touch of your hands be gentle
like the flower of the night.
Stand still, O Beautiful End,
for a moment, and say your last words in silence.
I bow to you and hold up my lamp
to light you on your way."

—Rabindranath Tagore, "Peace, My Heart"

"What we have once enjoyed we can never lose; all that we deeply love becomes a part of us."

—Helen Keller

"Unrealistically, I want to be done with grief. He died. Over. Next."

—KK

"Sometimes, no matter how much you want people to stay, you have to let them go."

—Tae Keller, *When You Trap a Tiger*

"The healing power of even the most microscopic exchange with someone who knows in a flash precisely what you're talking about because she experienced that thing too cannot be overestimated."

—Cheryl Strayed, *Tiny Beautiful Things*

"Be aware that when grief hits in all of its power, we instinctually try to resist the sense of overwhelm. But resistance to pain only serves to amplify it. Try sinking into it and feel it become more spacious. Allow it to wash over you and feel the strength return to your body and your mind. When you surrender to grief, you will discover that you are so much stronger than you ever imagined. Peace lies at the center of the pain, and although it will hurt, you will move through it a lot faster than if you distracted yourself with external outings."

—paraphrased from Elisabeth Kübler-Ross

"I'm not sure which is worse—the sharp, unbearable pain of the loss or the faint tingling that I know will eventually, and forever, follow."

—KK

"Go only as fast as your slowest part feels safe to go."

—Robyn Posin

"What could I learn from him to make his death have meaning and make me a better person through his undying influence on me?"

—KK

"Make it [grieving] mean something."

—Dani Shapiro

"Grief is not the enemy. Grief is here to heal you. Grief is your friend, and it has a beginning and an end."

—Kristine Carlson

"Grief never leaves you. It's always with you. In that sense, the tense of grief can be present and past combined."

—Mitchell Untch

"Never. We never lose our loved ones. They accompany us; they don't disappear from our lives. We are merely in different rooms."

—Paulo Coelho, *Aleph*

Keeping a Journal

Recently, I imagined what my life would be like if I had never kept a journal. The only upside I can think of is that I would have possibly spent more time experiencing present moments, since journaling is a private process of collection and recollection. But what I would *not* have represents a void that no amount of experience could ever fill.

- Without my journals, I would not have a sacred space devoted to reflection that has enabled me to process and integrate experience, the precursors to drawing meaning from it and using that meaning to better my life.

- Socrates said, "The unexamined life is not worth living," and had I not examined my life through journaling, I would not truly know myself.

- Put simply, a journal is a refuge, a sanctuary where you can express yourself, listen to yourself, and be yourself, giving yourself a place—a home base—to refresh yourself for the challenges life inevitably brings. Without my journals, I would be lost.

- Forgetting can be a salve, but remembering—especially through writing down what we recall so we can re-call it later when we need it—is, I believe, the key not only to not repeating history but also to personal growth. Without my journals, I would have remained stunted and would not be the person I am today.

If you have been considering starting a journal, the following quotations may inspire you to try. If you have journals that you put aside, you may feel encouraged to begin again, picking up where you left off. Similarly, if you want to deepen your practice, look here as well.

Don't be intimidated or think you have to journal in a certain way. I tend to be eclectic, pasting photos, making little drawings, and collecting images for collage. I don't write every day or feel it to be a discipline. Instead, when

I feel the urge to include something, I do. When I review my journals, often the dense, intense explorations of feelings and challenges are the hardest to reread. More enlightening are my dreams, new insights, and unfinished business. You may want to use your journals to highlight accomplishments, write tributes to people you have loved and lost, or record special days and things that surprised you because they turned out better than expected. Journaling is a highly individual process, and there is no right or wrong way to do it.

If, like me, you are a show-and-tell kind of person, you may wish to view the over 100 illustrations of actual journal pages included in my memoir, *Becoming Visible to Myself.* While organized and—not for the faint of heart—indexed according to the chapters of my life, they are also a mish-mosh, motley crew of words and images. As I wrote in my book:

> My inner Taskmaster is embarrassed they are so messy and wishes they could all be perfect, like a well-manicured English garden. My inner Poet, however, is delighted with each and every one, confident of the way they express their truth organically, like a sprawling yard of wildflowers.

Enough preamble, let's get to the quotations! The first batch is from my own writing about my journals and my process of keeping them; the second is drawn from those who have inspired me. I hope there is something here for everyone.

Keeping a journal has helped me in two ways: to value being introspective and to provide a container for my agony.

It didn't matter if I was working around the clock, there was always time to write in my journal.

Both writing and revisiting my journals has been a saving grace, a vehicle to help me process and deal with my awkward moments, disappointments, missteps, and grief.

My journals became a new venue for "Heartfelt Spaces," a term that has expanded to include activities that brought me joy, connection, and deep satisfaction.

What goes in my journals resonates with me; there is no need to analyze or debate.

For me, the act of journaling is an act of self-love.

Journaling has been my lifeline, and has helped me navigate my way through work, relationships, family, and therapy. It has been like a best friend, my comfort clothes, and a sacred space.

I finally saw myself in the mirror of my own writing. I couldn't deny the truth of what I had written.

I now have the ability to hear my fears and concerns. I may wish they'd go away, but I don't ignore them or beat myself up for their presence.

I finally had enough clues to connect the dots. I was becoming visible to myself, even if I wasn't going off into the sunset with a shiny new plan.

"Keeping a journal will absolutely change your life in ways you've never imagined."

—Oprah Winfrey

"Your journal will stand as a chronicle of your growth, your hopes, your fears, your dreams, your ambitions, your sorrows, your serendipities."

—Kathleen Adams

"All the noise in my brain. I clamp it to the page so it will be still."

—Barbara Kingsolver, *The Poisonwood Bible*

"The very act of writing it down made her realize how easy it would be to forget, how important it would be from now on to put everything, everything, down on paper."

—Donna Tartt, *The Little Friend*

"Write hard and clear about what hurts."

—attributed to Ernest Hemingway

"Writing bridges the inner and outer worlds and connects the paths of action and reflection."

—Christina Baldwin, *Life's Companion: Journal Writing as a Spiritual Practice*

"We write to taste life twice, in the moment and in retrospection."

—Anaïs Nin

"I write entirely to find out what I'm thinking, what I'm looking at, what I see, and what it means. What I want and what I fear."

—Joan Didion, *Let Me Tell You What I Mean*

"To pay attention, this is our endless and proper work."

—Mary Oliver, "Yes! No!"

"Don't bend, don't water it down, don't try to make it logical, don't edit your own soul according to the fashion."

—Anne Rice

"Fill your paper with the breathings of your heart."

—William Wordsworth

"I can shake off everything as I write; my sorrows disappear, my courage is reborn."

—Anne Frank, *The Diary of a Young Girl*

"There is no greater agony than bearing an untold story inside you."

—Maya Angelou, *I Know Why the Caged Bird Sings*

"In solitude we give passionate attention to our lives, to our memories, to the details around us."

—Virginia Woolf

"Writing is the only way I have to explain my own life to myself."

—Pat Conroy

"Everything in life is writable about if you have the outgoing guts to do it, and the imagination to improvise."

—Sylvia Plath, *The Unabridged Journals*

"Writing is medicine. It is an appropriate antidote to injury. It is an appropriate companion for any difficult change."

—Julia Cameron, *The Right to Write*

"In the journal I do not just express myself more openly than I could to any person; I create myself."

—Susan Sontag

"Everything I know about life I learned from the daily practice of sitting down to write."

—Dani Shapiro, *Still Writing: The Perils and Pleasures of a Creative Life*

"The journal is the ideal place of refuge for the inner self because it constitutes a counterworld; a world to balance the other."

—Joyce Carol Oates

"Whether you're keeping a journal or writing as a meditation, it's the same thing. What's important is you're having a relationship with your mind."

—Natalie Goldberg

Vulnerability Is Strength

Rather than offer a trite conclusion summarizing everything I've presented, I'd like to leave you with one of the most significant pieces of wisdom that flowed from my journaling:

112 ◆ Your Little Book of Wisdom

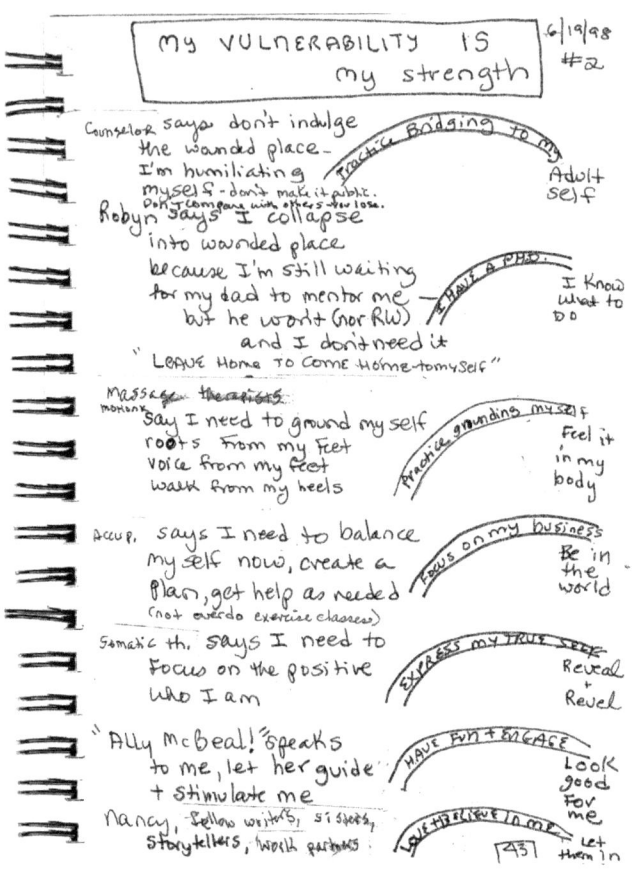

MY VULNERABILITY IS my strength — 6/19/98 #2

Counselor says don't indulge the wounded place — I'm humiliating myself - don't make it public. Don't compare with others—you lose.
Practice Bridging to my Adult self

Robyn says I collapse into wounded place because I'm still waiting for my dad to mentor me — but he won't (nor RW) and I don't need it
HAVE A PLAN. I know what to do

"LEAVE Home TO COME Home—to myself"

Massage therapists / motions say I need to ground myself roots from my feet voice from my feet walk from my heels
Practice grounding myself Feel it in my body

Acup. says I need to balance myself now, create a Plan, get help as needed (not overdo exercise classes)
Focus on my business Be in the world

Somatic th. says I need to focus on the positive who I am
Express my TRUE SELF Reveal + Revel

"Ally McBeal!" speaks to me, let her guide + stimulate me
HAVE FUN + ENGAGE Look good for me

Nancy, fellow writers, sisters, storytellers, work partners
JUST BELIEVE IN ME Let them in

[45]

www.ingramcontent.com/pod-product-compliance
Lightning Source LLC
Chambersburg PA
CBHW070644050426
42451CB00008B/296